Souls in Plain Clothes

Souls in Plain Clothes

Corrado Paina

Mansfield Press

Printed in Canada

Library and Archives Canada Cataloguing in Publication

Paina, Corrado, 1954-
Souls in plain clothes / Corrado Paina.

Poems.
ISBN 978-1-894469-37-1

I. Title.
PS8581.A484S69 2008 C811'.6 C2008-905894-1

Design: Denis De Klerck
Cover Photo: iStockphoto

The publication of *Souls in Plain Clothes* has been generously supported by the Canada Council for the Arts and the Ontario Arts Council.

ONTARIO ARTS COUNCIL
CONSEIL DES ARTS DE L'ONTARIO

Canada Council for the Arts
Conseil des Arts du Canada

Mansfield Press Inc.
25 Mansfield Avenue, Toronto, Ontario, Canada M6J 2A9
Publisher: Denis De Klerck
www.mansfieldpress.net

To Carlo and Franca

Contents

The grand tour

It was not inside us
it was not outside of us
it was the union
a feeding of each other

in life we were destined to fail
our aim was to stay away
always
unable to participate in the grand tour of life
we drew imaginary maps in our heart
it was really eccentric!
Such places!
we fed ourselves with landscapes
and people
learning that there was life with or without us

had I been paper
you would have been the pen
and vice versa
and so on ad infinitum
through all the dialectics of the world
until we would have understood
that it was not the arrival at the port
that divided us
but the end of planning impossible travels together

(to Luigi)

Our afternoon bed

like many years ago mother
we laid on the bed
on the same bed
in the same afternoon light

you fell asleep before me
your wrinkled eyelids
sealed forever the perpetual dream
of renewing time
the distant whine of the windlass
the remote whistle of the motorcycle
the abrupt slam of the shutter
at times interrupted our nap

this neighborhood goes to bed in the afternoon
the sun pushes our souls into hiding
this is the bed where you were dying
after years of forecasting death
your heart was finally surrendering

some bodies our bodies!
some souls our souls!
you woke up and caressed my hands
I had forgotten the embrace
you whispered to me with words of a mother
and I did not know the words of a son anymore

Carlo

"*respirare il padre*" (Salvo)

soldier in three wars
desert survivor and p.o.w.
and businessman in your second life
you rejected the medal of honour
(I have always loved this story – less the motivations)
when you found your way back
you knocked at mother's door
with no hair, fake teeth and perforated eardrums
you were so emaciated that she didn't recognize you
but you needed no disguise to hide your defeated face
surely you had high hopes for your son
I withdrew from war by wandering in the streets
I was a prisoner of a sorceress for more than 12 years
surely I had high expectations for the two of you
no I didn't become a doctor or a lawyer and no
I didn't become a priest
my friends collected the papers I left in their homes
with some stumbling verses
perhaps I meant to pay for my board
or just to leave a trail of crumbs
I was not able to carry you on my shoulders
outside the city in flames
my little poems are on your grave
renegade words for the death of another unknown soldier

I am just a gardener

your scent of life
disorients me with a cloud of guilt

I thought of withdrawing
when the banner of a future
black as the past
called me with its familiar sounds

I am not your father
I am just a gardener pruning darkness
watering your sleep with little poems
seeding passion in your mouth
picking words out of air

my son you will have contempt for me
but I have flown with you through a milky way
with a grateful heart and regretful eyes

just read me sometimes
when I am dead

And I am also a sentinel

your eyes are closing while voices
get distant and silence is your ghostly friend
you leave me here to live
with lucid knowledge of time

it is not your concern
how much time is left to me
even if you died because of the
ineffability of life

what a blasphemy!
and if statistics are right
I have twenty springs left
more or less

but you are still unaware of time
and you might forget me

I am just an ordinary sentinel
of the castle
I keep vigil over your sleep
and the world's
I am watching the plains
to alert the sleeping ones of the presence
of the foolish rules of life

because it is well known
though I am not going to tell you
that your sleep is just training
for life and the end of life
and the thought makes me light another cigarette
which according to the statistics
shortens my life
by one minute one day
one wish one orgasm
one lunch one taxi ride
one kiss (it shortens life too)
one rare and misogynous nightingale

(to Luca)

A depressed passenger at the last supper according to Peter Greenaway

the disease is developing
in the sensorial physiological weaving

the conceit is electric

the matter takes shapes and it undoes

the body is a defendant with no appeal
in a public trial

the genesis changes into the genetics
of an overseeing God
the disease of man
the indivisible
the philologically ineffable

Poem of the mother

has summer lingered with that vague stench of rubbish?
when the watermelon quenched you with a touch of sugar
is it still the summer of mirages of bucolic epiphanies?
of bicycles flying over the ditches?
of voices from the flock of birds far far away?
their whimsical syllables bouncing among the poplars?
not that you ever liked summer
you always praised spring
because summer lured reckless insects to the flowers of your dress
when those evenings whispered love
and you were listening to the disoriented animals
or were you confused by the sweat of your new body
before motherhood?
at last you could make shadows with the night lamp
in the nocturnal games with your sisters
laughing at your foolishness
the dead, if there's justice, are granted a return to youth
without work
without cry mama children
without husband
newly again new
who am I now? who am I for you?
do you remember when you were a child?
a question of a son who is not a son anymore
will you listen to my confession? could you again?
how many words will you hear?
and how much time has been given to you?
at last lucky you
time is no more
I mean the human time
original as the sin of living

I leave you my words

I leave you my words
they are weary and they have bad breath
I leave you my words
listen to them

I leave words
your youth will nourish
and they will grow stronger
because words can grow
and they can also age
and like birds that don't sing
they'll die of melancholy

like birds they have seen the world
I forgot them in damp cages
so I leave you my words
don't be afraid of their flight
they'll come back

they are mating in Samarkand or Thule
they'll bring you back the secret of music

(to Andrea)

The memory of India

It was not too long ago
or maybe it was a long time ago
but not enough to erase the memory
of a place where I have been
where the dream laid its body
where my hunger was terminated

In this place I felt my humanity
my strong and uncompromising flesh
I have never been to India
but I have memory of India

every tribunal in this land would condemn me
for pretending
I ask for the right to collect and treasure
the memories of places I have never been
of the man I have never been
of the dreams I have never had

Reconciliation of the first quarter

My adored one today you love me with one third of your love
I remember the force of your 100% love
a 100% love doesn't know how to count
it is not able to administer energies
nowadays love is 100% commitment and
1/3 of your love
you are at that point that loyalty
is about to outlive
to offset
the lost 2/3 of your love
stored in the trunk of that car
a 1991 Plymouth
our tears

At my age one courts

at my age one courts
the petals of life
one doesn't pick them any longer
is it true?
I mean at my age one finally
doesn't promise castles and diamonds anymore
time is already gone
and at my age one flirts with a flower
one flirts with the smell
flowers can be worse than human beings

(to Attilia, Claudia, Daniela and Francesca)

In a public washroom

A pisser is lost in a deathless dream

his dick can climb the mountain
can jump from the great wall of China

listen to that joyous outpouring
I don't see him but I can hear him
no problems, no work, no financial worries
and a thirteen year old prostate

me, I piss as if I was filing my income tax

Like Artaud used to say

I knew that I could have died that morning
since awakening my chest was in a tumult
there was the serenity of a just and balanced fear
the certainty of my end
that sky and that wind of that dawn
last companions and witnesses of my departure

a flavour of execution
the hollow atmosphere of pain and of shame
I was a bit sorry anyway for the lack of hope
of transubstantiation
all things considered I said to myself
it doesn't even hurt
the air smelled of sea and freedom
and it could not be by chance

therefore I got dressed
choosing the proper clothes
with the humbleness and the diligence of someone who
wakes up every morning and goes to work
who stops at the newsstand to scrounge stories foreign to him
before taking the bus and scrounging passengers' familiar stories
I left the lunch on a chair in the kitchen
I left the bed religiously made

for I was going to be *suicided*
like Artaud used to say
for a death without a fire escape
for an end without a panic door

there was no fog and the light was turning on
among the ashes of a boreal night
in the park I waited trying to catch maternal messages

paternal invitations
friendly shouts
sounds of failure
victory whispers and secrets of hissing memory

I am simply passing away
cordially
I said to myself
tears were veiling my sight
though my dignity was sheltered
while time was imprisoned by this embrace
between nothing and nothingness
I am alive!

Grazie dei fiori

In me the residuals
of picnics in the Dolomites
gold and pepper and scented kisses and stone
strawberries
sisters singing
a good boy picking flowers
spring mother
oak father
yes love but fear a lot of fear
a sneaky son
dreaming of leaving forever
dreaming of coming back as a conqueror
sated and respected
the record skips
a new song from "grazie dei fiori" to
"Coney Island baby"
streets Christmas shelters
tasteless kisses
at war
diving into forgetfulness
have I been a bad son ? no problem!
kisses flow again and words open their wings
mother is swallowed by pain
father is sailing to silence
sisters pick the last flowers
I compile a list of accomplishments:
two children
a woman
two orphan sisters
a full time job
some ambitions
several friends

I don’t know why I am living here and
I wouldn’t know where else I could live either
I write poetry
I can only hope that I will not outlive my kids
and that a thunderstorm will wash me away painlessly

Planning death

At what time does one die?
At what time will you die?

On a hot afternoon at 2:33 p.m.
with the sound of a ball bounced by someone
killing time

or on a winter morning at 6:03 a.m.
after a night of pain and fever
someone will smoke a cigarette on
your behalf drinking coffee
looking inconsistently through the window

so at what time does one die?

at 11:49 when the broth reaches the edge of the pot
freeing bovine spirits and/or avian scents

or when the palm tree bows to the whistle
of the belligerent wind
and the sand grazes the eyes
of the fisherman
or the boy squeezes his hand
checking his pale knuckles
in the solitude of his room

you will not die tomorrow
you will not die one day
because you died yesterday

you didn't know and you didn't imagine it
on those sunny days when

rays and children played in the field or
you were watching the sky on the balconies flowering the city

you suspected when the bird had sung
and the snow drop came out of its white shell

it happened on a Monday
you were going to the office
and you ended up checking into the hospital
you talked with the staff on duty
fool! do not be so grateful!
they did what they could
nothing
they told you that everything was fine
but you were already dead
you were so grateful, you were full of happy tears
an outpouring of praise for life
you came back home
thinking that you would change your life
like the movie director used to say
died at 30
buried at 70

(to Giorgio Caproni and to George A. Romero)

The body of the writer

In the morning of each morning I leave my body on the couch
I don't need my body to write

In the night I join the halves
and clean sheets of words cover me with the sleep of oblivion

nothing hurts more than a dismembered soul
calling for the assembly of lost voices
nothing is warmer than the singing of solitude

at last I close my eyes weary
of a life of writing
at last

but words don't warm
words ache in the transcending night

Under the tree of heaven

children these are somebody else's words
that I hope you will understand today or tomorrow
I will long for the sounds of your tongues
I will long for your senseless crying

dinner is ready!
let me announce
this is the last supper of a writer
who was not able to understand your purity

I'll separate from poetry
children all the statues have been mutilated
their heads looking at the sun

their chiseled features
never appeared so beautiful
children you have no idea
of the fatal epilogue

before you receive a notice I want to tell you
that poetry and I
are no longer lovers

she dumped me for any faithful partner
who remembers her birthday

as per our telephone conversation
sex is non-existent
communication is disruptive and destructive

poetry and I sadly announce the departure of words
from this banquet
friends and family express their deepest condolences

...the terms of an agreement to separate were approved by both entities starting today.

" While these issues have caused great pain for many people, the agreement allows us to move forward on separate paths."

Notes for a documentary

In a documentary that remembers the dead
the pictures must be in colour
the dead must be remembered in living colours
the living ones should be shot in black and white
the documentary starts in white and it changes to grey like the
skin of a sick human being
or it can start from black and change to white
the documentary ends with bad deeds as credits

Frame

I am a painting
I am a landscape
still life
muscular fatigue
fatigue of system
and all the natural and acrylic drugs
crash against the white waves of the surface
I am always a still life
of sky
of earth
of fire

(to Sandro)

The persimmon, my phalanstery

Tonight mother I will eat the fruit of autumn
at home
the prize for my return from school
because I didn't escape
because I have learnt what you wanted me
to learn

there is a stage of rottenness
that smells of apples and strawberries
it sings before death
it is the pleasure of selling my soul

tonight the persimmon
is the shrine
of my surrendering
tonight I will sleep golden dreams of a phalanstery
where there are no good and bad children
no good and bad deeds
where everyone is awarded a persimmon for his actions

(to Massimo "Macio")

Fruit basket (canestra di frutta)

(I met Caravaggio on a subway car)

This is only the beginning of a still life
there's death
                              and corruption
there's the magistry
                                   of life
and there's something more
                                                            the deceit
like the background of a wall
which stands witness
to death in motion
chipping and staining
the still life
incapable of stopping the course
                                                            of decay

We believed that tears could end

that the dry river was awaiting
the rain of autumn
but the storm doesn't stop
swelling the clouds
the wind striking the pines

the blue sea is indifferent to us
the gurgling of the stream is chattering to us
contemptuous in the shrine
the sun a pagan god burning whimsically

there's so much to do in life
to ostracize the spirits of the dead
more alive more real more impermeable to their pain

Father

I can see
with your eyes
plains ending their race in the womb of mountains

restful seas like shadows of cobalt
in the corneas of the earth
things that you loved to watch
from the bridge of the ship

the sky giving birth at dawn
the half asleep snow drop

with your eyes
tears will not have weight anymore
my mind will walk to you
in a field laid fallow

(to Vanni , to Erio, and to M. Masud R. Khan)

I don't care about animals

I have never been crazy about animals
I like horses, elephants and whales
I hate dogs, ideologically
I am not crazy about cats
though I like them ideologically
I have animals in my body
there is a hummingbird in my eyes
and one can feel the graze of his wings
no, I am not an angel
there's a hummingbird in my deeds
in my thoughts
you might notice it, see it, but
you cannot catch it
I love a dog, Spencer, because he is a great host
he introduces me to his friends
and he waits for my fortune cookie
we don't hunt together
we are just aging together
we listen to our approaching diseases
he is like a bartender
who listens to me
as part of his job
until we go home
on separate paths
my children are my pets
ideologically I sympathize with their love for me
they love me because I have a long nose and because
of my barrel chest and because
my prominent stomach is their playing field
but they are also forgetful when I am away
as long as there's somebody

their mother
my woman
she was with me in my previous lives
I was with her in her previous lives
her bones for me are the bones of the architecture
of shelter and abandonment
her jaws are banks seen from afar
I will tell you later about her shoulders and her calves
and her mouth which has the same energy of a sex athlete and a
renowned attorney
her eyes would force me to speak and write
and write and speak to audiences
there's a Mediterranean potion in them
yes there are waves but also the meadow and the stone
the olive tree and the cliff
the sky fallen into the sea
there's Icarus and Sisyphus
there's arrogance and punishment
there's chasteness and compassion
they quench their thirst at the
fountain of legend
she has the fragility of the prototype
and the gambling smile of the unconscious newcomer in the road

I stumble and mumble for your creation
as you stumble in my ranting
if I had real hands able to shape objects and fruit
you wouldn't be different
you have been a watermelon in the hottest
and blinding summer
you have been a grain of sand at the first convention
of the desert
the echo in the cave of prophecies, the prophecy itself
and a paintbrush, a note and, because you have your faults too,

the jaguar ambushing the toucan
have you been a wave?
the incarnation of a soul
embarking and stowing
the regret and the peace of departure?
before you I was asking for silence
being a stone fornicating with many millions
in the limbs of the Alps
under a vault of bodies
longing for the water or the rain
if I am a diamond for you
I also come from a crater
but I have been fast
so fast that no runner could dream of it
let me introduce myself
I have been a corpse in the rain
I have been an ant and a dictionary
of another language
I carry the fall, the ink and a strong stomach
I bring laziness and vanity
you carry the sight, the murmur, the trunk
and you bring inertia and capacity
we all had previous lives and the memory of them
keeps us unfinished
Andrea washes her teeth with the disdain and the disgust
of one plunging the bleeding sword in a river
Luca is testing the inexplicable teachings of growth
if they are animals it is because of their uncompromising ignorance

meet me at the oxymoron of peace
and of war
meet me at a safe distance
where and when my guilt rests

dawn ought to have your eyes
fog ought to have your smile
leaves ought to have your skin

I kneel in front of this world
which exists only for me
and I pray it remains mine

(to Deborah)

It's me, don't you recognize me ?

No other way to tell you about my love
than shape it in the breathing snow
so it bites me, to remind me that under the whiteness
there's always flesh

I outlived you

thank you for leaving discreetly
before me
thank you for not coming back
for not seducing me with a family portrait
for not burying me with grievances
the reminder of your mortal sin
mutated on thanksgiving day

thank you God for darkness
the real one
without bonfires and
selenic blazes

Last station

Terrified by the whistle of departure we let them leave
we let them slip into deep holes into gelid waters
we segregate them into memories

there are more skies to conquer
there are more dreams to embrace
the dead should forgive us

(to all the friends of Bar Curci)

Souls in plain clothes

Carlo,

on your behalf
I was searching
through the waters
of this peremptory injury
in the earth
and in an armistice between
life and death I wrote you
a poem, a letter
that you will never read
(though not everyone will agree)

I was sitting on a crust of a rock
among many people looking for whales
the tail, the flipper, the spurt

you would have spent hours breathing loudly
and praising the smell of this salty river
why are all these seekers here
stalking a miracle
to be healed
to be first to spot the whales?

the opposite bank is so far that
I feel I am still banned
from crossing
I am alive Carlo,
and I can see the whales with your eyes
and your name is on the waters
each wave carrying a name
the names of the dead
at last we see

a spraying wave
an effervescent soul knocking at our memory
are all the waves souls in disguise?
traveling souls in plain clothes?
waves in flesh and bones?

we all stand trying to recognize
our lost dear ones
all united and yet alone

Tadoussac
August 2006

(to Stefania and Emilia)

Something like that

Stefano this morning in a dream
you whispered the most beautiful poem to me

it was winter 1982
you were walking along the street
in worn clothes
mumbling and speaking to yourself
grazed by stores and people

I remember fall 1971
the gardens of via Guastalla
sanctuary of our escapes from school

we sat on a bench and
you placed your Ulysses
over the dead leaves
I moored at the second page of
curlingreenwaves
or something like that

Stefano this morning in a dream
you told me the most beautiful poem
asta onda rabba ti
or something like that

this morning we started again
after thirty years to share poems
that no one can hear but us
the virus is only ours

(to Stefano in a dream)

The sanctuary of civilization

Child and dog are playing
the fire is crackling
life is smiling in intervals
insensitive to guilt and memory
life repeats its journey

the repetition of the history of men
is like placing your ear on the mouth of the shell
nobody can trust the voice of this ocean
nobody can believe that our whisper is caged inside
nobody but us

Training for 3000

having missed the opportunity of being adequate
I am training for a millennium that I will not see
which will not care about me
centennial plans suit me properly
I am more malleable more flexible
complying to the rules of a marriage by proxy
in the year 3000 I could also be happy

To my parents

Perhaps the reader will be wondering how a book can be dedicated to parents? Another dedication to parents... was it guilt? Was the writer a bad son in the past and is now confessing his repentance with his dedication? And who were these two human beings? Were they good or bad people? Did they deserve a book? And how come the eyes of the writer were blinded by mediocrity, thanking parents and forgetting the deeds, the people he met, the places he visited, the historical events that brought him to write the book? Why not dedicate the book to all the writers that overcame solitude and poverty and above all anonymity? Why not dedicate the book to his first cigarette? Or to anything that was not about the rhetoric of parenthood?

I always look for my name in dedications, in the list of acknowledgements, even if the book was published before my birth. And I will always be grateful to the writer that challenges me with a long list of unknown human beings and animals, or flowers or clouds.

Dedication is beyond time as though time is unknown or time is lost in the whirlpool of names and lives that are gone forever.

This book is dedicated to Carlo and Franca. Both names mean free person. Carlo and Franca, a businessman and a teacher. Actually a lieutenant in the navy and a country girl. In fact a dreamer and a pragmatist. Actually...

Thirst

Ishmael asked – Father, why are men building another museum?
God replied – to segregate art, to imprison its beauty, to forbid her from flying away; true art will be able to reach heaven, the other will lay in the museums
(anonymous)

If the form vanishes, its root is eternal
(Mario Merz – Peggy Guggenheim Museum – Venice)

Embrace the walls

Over these roofs a muezzin could embrace the flames of sunset
in the radiant city so many democratic ears could vibrate with the sounds of diversity

the bells of the mass could orchestrate the flight of the seagulls
and too many could praise the urban legend of the global village
where neighbourhoods assemble to sing paeans to coexistence and tolerance

here they are: the ecstatic assembly of the endorsers
and the insatiable scavengers of ethnic food

the repetition of the whipping of the crucified man
the remake of the wreath of the conqueror
will make the neighbors feel at home

the walls set the time of nostalgia and displacement
the gates open to the mysticism of the old country
all these rivers of belief collect in a calm sea of righteousness
their streams itemized in hymns to government policies
boxed and packaged in a sea shell
that whispers the same word: pride pride pride

there's a juice in the flowers that only children
can drink
we are banned from bringing it to our lips
this is not what you would call prayer
this is not what you would call a miracle
and this is not because of original sin

champions of freedom and those who know the rationale
behind everything

advocates of multicultural transubstantiation
embrace the walls!

Can you hear a voice that lures us slowly to neutrality
and tolerance?
It's a refrain that reels off many warnings
and resembles the Pied Piper whose sounds
push us like mice into the invisible Lake Ontario
and we drown dragged down by concrete neologisms
Multiaccessmultiaddictmultiadvocatemultiarbitratormultiathlete
multiballotmultibarriomultibathroommultibombmulticavitymulti-
Canadianmultichallengedmultichannelmulticitizenmulticleaning
multiclinicmulticoffeemulticondominiummulticulturalmulticunt
multidisciplinarymultidrugmultieducationmultiemailmultiemis-
sionmultiethnicmultiexclusionmultiexhibitionmultiexitmultiexter-
minatormultifacemultifairmultifaithmultifinemultifuckmultinsur-
ancenumbermultigallerymultigarbagemultigendermultigentrifica-
tionmultiglobalmultiguidelinemultihomelessmultijailmultilandlord-
multinclusionmultintegrationmultilingualmultilovermultinative-
multimortgagemultineighbourhoodmultipersonalitymultiplanning-
multipoetrymultipridemultiproductmultiracemultischlepmultisex-
multisheltermultisoldiermultitonguemultitolerantmultivictim
multivoicemail

Our city of backyards
of sanctuary of solitudes and familistic dreams
is plastered over with banners and posters of coexistence
gnawed by the rodents of tradition

souls hidden in basements
skyscraping souls in forgotten barrios

tenants are injected by city officials
steroids of rhetoric to fight
linguistic weaknesses and isolation illnesses

we are unfinished humans
in an unfinished city
where the wind blows the unleashed message
of opportunity and pride
pride in growing here
pride in loving this land
and despite the opposition of a municipal council
all this pride should be incinerated
for the most exhilarating emission
for the ultimate mass event
that will overcome the drums of Caribana
the shouts of Pride day
the laments of the procession
the assemblies of tribes
where the folkloristic gathering
mercilessly shows all our inabilities to pray alone

mother Toronto
embracing latitudes and parallels
and feeding us with limits and regulations
I strip you of your praised pride
I kill your ambassador
you are just a wide naked body
of blind residential serenity
and your crown of gold and diamond
is just a wall of condos
studded with plexiglass and concrete

it's your culture that spells
listen
it's your memory that moors
listen to the sea shell

if we all return to our
point of departure
this city would cry from Bay Street
to 905

embrace the walls!
these breasts of brick, concrete and metal
need your tears
embrace the walls!

what is civic aesthetic without vanity?
this proselytism of an urban gospel
of a global falling in love
with the city
is just coy voyeurism
at the orgies of high bohemians
could you fall in love with the veins of the metropolis
scarred by motors?
with the mute alleys of suburbs inhabited by
sleeping machines?

build a tower in Scarborough
erect a museum
put fashion in your window
confine the mayor over there
3 months a year
in distant Scarborough
and three months a year at Jane and Finch

mother Toronto it is time to evict art
time for the artists to expel paradigms

time for the artists to abandon museums
and galleries
if this is the place
we are the place
where we can bury
the metaphors under the snow
the snow of the Greater Tundra Area

embrace the walls
embrace the humility of the one who carries no history
the unknown citizen
doesn't need a monument
it is the artist that needs relocation

only the poet will not reuse reduce recycle
his words
only the poet will incinerate his soul
and poetry will finally reach the sky
embrace the walls!

(to Pier Giorgio)

Madeleine

– would you care for a madeleine?
says the lady that brings my cocoon of sweetness on a tray
madam, I have no connection with this madeleine
and a cannolo wouldn't do the job
and I won't take the tunnel to childhood
no I am not afraid of the snake that will bite me
his venom is innocuous like his hissing
while I am drinking coffee and smoking
the last mountain of glass is swelling
I should leave again
because I don't know where this pouring of concrete will end
I can see where art will be frozen
I can see the artist behind the window enjoying
the perfect solstice of a quiet man
who was poor and angry once
and now he wants to park his legacy of nails and wood
let me taste a nail
let me hear the hammer
let me breathe this air of sweat and dream
of expectation and waiting
before dust and time imprisons
his soul
if the past is the same as the future
and the present is noise
what can a poor sweet madeleine do?

The eviction of the insolvent artist

I had not thought death had undone so many.
(The Waste Land – T.S. Eliot)

The fallen are many
only the lucky ones
and the most eloquent prevail
in the pantheistic city
art is a corpse exhibited prudishly in squares and colosseums
the industry of the corpse prospers
subjugated by municipal ruling

public art believes it exists
architecture believes it exists
museums believe they are real
artists believe that language can reach the sky

there are no barricades
along the *decumanus* and the *cardo*
to stop the pompous stagecoaches of art

another museum
another temple for fast religions
municipal councils open museums and casinos
and churches temples stadiums
but we will return to this matter...

Toronto you don't need perennial buildings
your story is mercurial
your human element is immortal
it is not museumable
museums are not the voice of air
the air that freezes decay
the air that gives death to art
the air that gives life to art

The lake is over us

nomadic water pipes run underground
gentrified citizens assemble at the
ballots of unregistered grievances
somebody sees suddenly the vanished lake

there was a lake at the beginning of time
with gigantic trees

there was a time that you
could smell the lake weed early in the morning

buildings gated the community of
sirens and nymphs and gods

the impending skies
and the waters are only reflected
for the joy of a few
by the glass of the towers

the city thought it was closer to god
and over the city waves and boats were flying
it was easy for dreams to sail upward
it was easy for the rain to swell and fall

sometimes triggered by a crosswind
we feel the urgency of looking for water
when heaven parachutes a rainbow over the buildings

sometimes there are identifiable symptoms of alertness
when a passage appears through the greed of concrete
and our inexplicable thirst is quenched by the lake

by its mumbling waves
by the moored island
by the lure of distant lands

there's still a homeless person that remembers
the lake
and wants to run for mayor

The radiant city and the other

In the radiant city the architecture disappears and appears salvifically
by chance
to be seen is everything in the other city
these buildings are public shelters of art

Van Gogh's bleeding ear is displayed in squares
in the *pronaos* of financial institutions
the anodyne flesh of global obesity
is inviting citizens to dream sweetly
in the other city the air is mute
art spaces are allocated
corpses are dropped here and there
like sleeping homeless people
and as for homeless people
few stop to give a coin
nobody talks
the multitude runs away hastily

in the other city art commutes to oblivion

(to Alfredo and Mario)

Alternative energy

Gangs gather on terraces
in undergrounds
and in malls to strategize the invasion
this is not home
our soul is a broken window
a cockroach life along the pipes
of dark basements

their shadows touch
the banks of our soul
only for a moment
it is energy into waste
none of us is recyclable

Thirst

Goodbye mother
I am leaving soon
Vado fuori all'aperto
there's a city in ferment and there's a city where
we are fermenting
it's thirst
in ferment over my residence
in ferment over my allegiance
in ferment over my being in ferment
fermented by pride
fermented with pride
I am thirsty for nothingness
I am thirsty for oblivion

I am nowhere close I am nowhere here I am nowhere there
I am nowhere certifiable
I am nowhere identifiable
it's thirst
in between identities
in between waves
in between epochs
in between routes
in between parties
uttermost oblivious thirst
uttermost recalcitrant thirst
uttermost separated
uttermost irreprehensible
as far as I am disposable
as far as I am an "ur-stowaway"
this is not about hyphenation it is about annihilation
from countries
from languages

I am no one here I was no one before being here
free at last and a prisoner
free of all my selves

if I am something (and not someone)
I am a dual language writer
bi-impotent more than bi-sexual
I cannot hide my language
I cannot marry their language
I am multi-tongued
thirsty for all the dicks and cunts of
literature
all the springs and rivers and streams of
poetry
it's thirst

Nostalgia

in Europe I could have injected
the ignorance of borders
or caged the sun
among relics of horizons
I could have died three times and
perjured and again traveled and flown
and stopped
here I close my eyes
they are biforas at night
in this impalpable organoleptic and north American suggestion

The legend of downloading

If I was there
I was unwittingly
training in the dogma of free choice
weaning from the supreme proletarian design

after forty days I came back with two truths
ignorance is a solid justification
misery was before poverty

then they downloaded me
into biodegradable files
and words faded
only the virus stood immortal

The sunken city

The walls seal
universal chatter
screams of planets
whispers of stars

the pigeons ford the blue
from the temple to the sky
from the sky to the temple
a thrill of wings echo
like the stroke of immortality

Postscript

By Christopher Hume

In a world grown weary of noisy narcissism and the cacophony of the crowd, Corrado Paina's poetry is an exquisite and welcome reminder of the lost art of reflection.

Despite the intensely personal nature of his poems – perhaps because of it – they are as universal as they are intimate. Who amongst us has not felt with Paina that the most profound insights can emerge from the most ordinary, even mundane, events?

His poems read as a series of despatches; sent not from the battlefield, of course, but the everyday world of work, friends and family life. As Paina's words make clear, however, whether we realize it or not, meaning is always there, just below the surface or just around the corner, it reveals itself, but only to those who recognize it.

That is the poet's great gift, as crucial today as ever, though perhaps never so undervalued as in the 21st century. Ours is a primarily visual age. We prefer images to words. We have replaced the page with the screen – whether television or computer.

But reading Paina's poems, one can't help but sense they were snatched from thin air, from non-existence, not laboured over for days on end, word by word, until perfection was achieved. To me, this smacks of lines scrawled on the back of envelopes in the middle of the afternoon, or early in the morning. It smacks of grabbing the idea before it vanishes into the ether from which it came. It is a hit-and-miss process, but then what art form isn't? And isn't this exactly what creativity is about? It lies not in the hope of perfection, but in taking the chance, risking it all in the hope of expressing the inexpressible.

"we are unfinished humans," Paina writes, "in an unfinished city/ where the wind blows the unleashed message/of opportunity and pride...."

Thus Paina's poetry forms a record of the human voyage towards completion. As he well understands, the point is not that we never arrive, but that the journey is one that leads to knowledge, awareness and, occasionally, wisdom.

That word – wisdom – is not one Paina would use in connection with his work; it would make him cringe. But in fact, through the writing of poetry, he seeks nothing less. Wisdom, after all, does not reside in an accumulation of facts; it is an attitude, an approach, a way of looking at things.

As another poet, T.S.Eliot once wrote, "The end of our exploring will be to arrive where we started and see the place for the first time." Come to think of it, Homer was saying much the same thing.

For Paina, who as Executive Director of the Italian Chamber of Commerce in Toronto has brought the time-honoured tradition of the poet-diplomat into the 21st century, it is work that seems to provide the sense of stability, connection and contemplation so hard to come by in a life spent travelling.

But just as poetry is a cultural construct, home is an emotional one. In Paina's poems the two collide harmoniously if not always happily.

After five books with Mansfield Press and several books and chapbooks with small publishing houses and fabulous artists in Italy, Corrado Paina still feels the desire to write